Copyright © 2020 by Jessica M

All rights reserved. No part of this publication may be reproduced, distributed, or transmitted in any form or by any means, including photocopying, recording, or other electronic or mechanical methods, without the prior written permission of the publisher, except in the case of brief quotations embodied in critical reviews and certain other noncommercial uses permitted by copyright law

Contents

Everything You Need to Know About Diverticulitis 6

Symptoms of diverticulitis 7

Causes of diverticulitis 8

Diagnosis of diverticulitis 9

Treatment for diverticulitis 12

Dietary changes 13

Medication 14

Other procedures 15

Surgery for diverticulitis 15

Bowel resection with anastomosis 16

Bowel resection with colostomy 16

Diet and diverticulitis 17

Home remedies for diverticulitis 18

Meckel's diverticulitis 19

Using a colonoscopy to diagnose diverticulitis 21

Preventing diverticulitis 22

Risk factors for diverticulitis 23

Family history 24

Low levels of vitamin D 24

Diverticulitis vs. diverticulosis 26

Diverticulitis and alcohol 30

Takeaway 31

Foods to Avoid If You Have Diverticulitis 32

What foods should I avoid if I have an acute bout of diverticulitis? 34

High-FODMAP foods 34

High-fiber foods 36

What foods should I eat if I have diverticulitis?.......... 39

Low-fiber foods 40

Clear liquid diet 41

Does a high-fiber diet reduce risk of diverticulitis?...... 43

Talk with your doctor.. 45

Diverticulitis Surgery.. 47

How do I prepare for this surgery? 51

How is this surgery done? 52

How to Eat (and Recover from) a Low-Fiber Diet 59

What's a low-fiber diet? 59

What can you eat on a low-fiber diet?....................... 61

Need a starting point? 66

Why is a low-fiber diet beneficial?............................ 67

Everything You Need to Know About Diverticulitis

What is it?

Although it was rare before the 20th century, diverticular disease is now one of the most common health problems in the Western world. It's a group of conditions that can affect your digestive tract.

The most serious type of diverticular disease is diverticulitis. It can cause uncomfortable symptoms and, in some cases, serious complications. If left untreated, these complications can cause long-term health problems.

Read on to learn more about diverticulitis, including its causes, symptoms, treatment options, and how your diet might affect your risk of developing it.

Symptoms of diverticulitis

Diverticulitis can cause symptoms ranging from mild to severe. These symptoms can appear suddenly or they can develop gradually over several days.

Potential symptoms of diverticular disease include:

- pain in your abdomen

- bloating

- diarrhea

- constipation

If you develop diverticulitis, you might experience:

- constant or severe pain in your abdomen

- nausea and vomiting

- fever and chills

- blood in your stool

- bleeding from your rectum

Abdominal pain is the most common symptom of diverticulitis. It will mostly likely occur in the lower left side of your abdomen. But it can also develop in the right side of your abdomen.

If you develop any of the above symptoms, such as vomiting or blood in your stool, it may be a sign of a serious complication from diverticulitis or another condition. Call your doctor right away.

Causes of diverticulitis

Diverticular disease develops when pouches form along your digestive tract, typically in your colon (large intestine). These pouches are known as diverticula. They form when weak spots in your intestinal wall balloon outward.

Diverticulitis happens when diverticula become inflamed and in some cases infected. This can occur when feces or partially digested food blocks the opening of the diverticula.

There's no single known cause of diverticular disease. Instead, experts believe that multiple genetic and environmental factors likely contribute to its development.

Diagnosis of diverticulitis

To diagnose diverticulitis, your doctor will likely ask you about your symptoms, health history, and any medications that you take. They'll likely perform a physical exam to check your abdomen for tenderness or, if they need more information, a digital rectal exam to check for rectal bleeding, pain, masses, or other problems.

Several other conditions can cause symptoms that are similar to diverticulitis. To rule out other conditions and check for signs of diverticulitis, your doctor might order one or more tests.

Tests can include:

• abdominal ultrasound, abdominal MRI scan, abdominal CT scan, or abdominal X-ray to create pictures of your gastrointestinal (GI) tract

• colonoscopy to examine the inside of your GI tract

• stool test to check for infections, such as Clostridium difficile

- urine test to check for infections

- blood tests to check for signs of inflammation, anemia, or kidney or liver problems

- pelvic exam to rule out gynecological problems in women

- pregnancy test to rule out pregnancy in women

If you have diverticulitis, these exams and tests can help your doctor learn if it's uncomplicated or complicated.

More than 75 percentTrusted Source of diverticulitis cases are uncomplicated, leaving about 25 percent to develop complications.

These complications can include:

- abscess, an infected pocket that's filled with pus

- phlegmon, an infected area that's less well-confined than an abscess

- fistula, an abnormal connection that can develop between two organs or between an organ and the skin

- intestinal perforation, a tear or hole in the intestinal wall that can allow the contents of your colon to leak into your abdominal cavity, causing inflammation and infection

- intestinal obstruction, a blockage in your intestine that can stop stool from passing

Treatment for diverticulitis

The treatment that your doctor prescribes for diverticulitis will depend on how severe your condition is.

Uncomplicated diverticulitis can typically be treated at home. Your doctor might encourage you to make changes to your diet. In some cases, they might prescribe medications including antibiotics.

If you develop complications from diverticulitis, you'll probably need to visit a hospital for treatment. You may be given fluids and antibiotics through an intravenous (IV) line. Depending on the type of complication, you might need to undergo surgery or another procedure.

Dietary changes

To give your digestive system a chance to rest and recover, your doctor might suggest avoiding solid foods and following a clear-liquid diet for a few days.

If your symptoms are mild or have started to improve, you may be able to try eating low-fiber foods until your condition gets better. As your condition improves, your doctor will likely encourage you to add more high-fiber foods to your snacks and meals.

Medication

To reduce pain or discomfort from diverticulitis, your doctor might recommend over-the-counter pain medications, such as acetaminophen (Tylenol).

If they suspect that you have an infection, they'll prescribe antibiotics to treat it. These include:

- metronidazole (Flagyl, Flagyl ER)

- amoxicillin

- moxifloxacin

It's important to take your full course of prescribed antibiotics, even if your symptoms improve after the first few doses.

Other procedures

If you develop a complicated case of diverticulitis that can't be treated through diet and medication alone, your doctor might recommend one of the following procedures:

• needle drainage, where a needle is inserted into your abdomen to drain an abscess of pus

• surgery to drain an abscess of pus, repair a fistula, or remove infected segments of the colon

Surgery for diverticulitis

If you experience multiple episodes of diverticulitis that can't be effectively managed with dietary changes and medications, your doctor might recommend surgery. Surgery may also be used to treat complications from diverticulitis.

There are two main types of surgery used to treat diverticulitis.

Bowel resection with anastomosis

During a bowel resection with anastomosis, a surgeon removes infected segments of your colon and reattaches the healthy segments to each other.

Bowel resection with colostomy

In a bowel resection with colostomy, the surgeon removes infected sections of your colon and attaches the end of the healthy section to an opening in your abdomen, known as a stoma.

Both procedures can be performed as open surgery or laparoscopic surgery. Learn more about the types of surgery that can be used to treat diverticulitis.

Diet and diverticulitis

Experts aren't yet sure about the role that diet plays in diverticulitis. There are no particular foods that everyone with diverticulitis has to avoid. But you might find that certain foods make your condition better or worse.

During an acute attack of diverticulitis, your doctor might encourage you to reduce your fiber intake for a while. They might advise you to avoid solid foods altogether and stick to a clear-liquid diet for a few days. This can give your digestive system a chance to rest.

As your symptoms improve, your doctor might encourage you to eat more high-fiber foods. Some studies have linked high-fiber diets to reduced risk of diverticulitis. Other studiesTrusted Source have examined possible benefits of dietary or supplemental fiber for diverticular disease, but are still unsure of the role fiber should play.

Your doctor might also encourage you to limit your consumption of red meat, high-fat dairy products, and refined grain products. A large cohort study found that people who follow a diet that's rich in these foods are more likely to develop diverticulitis than people who eat a diet rich in fruits, vegetables, and whole grains.

Diet can play a role in managing diverticulitis and your overall digestive health. Take a moment to learn about some of the foods that might affect your symptoms.

Home remedies for diverticulitis

Home remedies for diverticulitis mostly consist of making dietary changes, but there are a few other options that may be helpful for symptoms and digestive health.

Some studies have found that certain strains of probiotics might help relieve or prevent symptoms of diverticulitis. More research is needed to assess the potential benefits and risks of using probiotics to treat diverticulitis.

Certain herbs or supplements might also have benefits for your digestive health. However, there's currently little research to support the use of herbal remedies for diverticulitis.

Meckel's diverticulitis

Diverticular disease usually affects adults. But in rare cases, babies are born with diverticula. When this happens, it's known as Meckel's diverticulum. If the diverticula become inflamed, it's called Meckel's diverticulitis.

In some cases, Meckel's diverticulum doesn't cause noticeable effects. In other cases, it can cause symptoms such as:

- abdominal pain

- nausea

- vomiting

- bloody stool

- bleeding from the rectum

If you suspect that your child might have diverticulitis, make an appointment with their doctor.

Using a colonoscopy to diagnose diverticulitis

If you have symptoms of diverticulitis, your doctor might encourage you to have a colonoscopy once the acute episode resolves. This procedure can help confirm a diagnosis of diverticulitis or another condition that causes similar symptoms, such as ulcerative colitis or Crohn's disease.

During a colonoscopy, your doctor will thread a flexible scope into your rectum and colon. They can use this scope to examine the inside of your colon. They can also use it to collect tissue samples for testing.

To help you feel more comfortable during this procedure, you will be sedated beforehand.

In some cases, your doctor might learn that you have diverticula during a routine colonoscopy. If the diverticula aren't inflamed, infected, or causing symptoms, you probably won't need treatment.

Preventing diverticulitis

More research is needed to learn what causes diverticular disease, including diverticulitis. Currently, experts believe that multiple factors play a part. Some of your potential risk factors may be modified through lifestyle changes.

For example, it might help to:

- maintain a healthy body weight

- eat a diet that's high in fiber

- limit your consumption of saturated fat

- get enough vitamin D

- get regular exercise

- avoid cigarette smoke

These prevention strategies can also help promote good overall health.

Risk factors for diverticulitis

One of the main risk factors for diverticulitis is age. Older people are more likely than younger people to develop diverticulitis. It commonly occursTrusted Source in men under 50 and women ages 50 to 70.

But people who develop diverticula at a younger age may be more likely to experience diverticulitis. Younger people are also more likelyTrusted Source to be admitted to a hospital if they have diverticulitis than older people.

According to a review of research published in 2018, other potential risk factors for diverticulitis include:

Family history

Two large twin studies have found that genetics play a role in diverticular disease. The authors estimate that roughly 40 to 50 percent of the potential risk of diverticular disease is hereditary.

Low-fiber diet

Some research has linked low-fiber diets to increased risk of diverticulitis. However, other studies have found no link between dietary fiber intake and this disease.

Low levels of vitamin D

One studyTrusted Source suggests that people with higher levels of vitamin D might have a lower risk for getting diverticulitis. More research is needed to understand the potential link between vitamin D and this condition.

Obesity

Several studies have found that people with higher body mass index and larger waists are at increased risk of diverticulitis.

It's possible that obesity raises the risk of diverticulitis by changing the balance of bacteria in your gut, but more research is needed to understand the role that this plays.

Physical **inactivity**

Some studiesTrusted Source have found that physically active people are less likely than inactive people to develop diverticulitis. However, other research has found no link between exercise and this condition.

Using nonsteroidal anti-inflammatory drugs (NSAIDS) or smoking

Regular use of aspirin, ibuprofen, or other NSAIDs may raise your risk of diverticulitis.

Smokers are also more likely than nonsmokers to develop diverticular disease, including diverticulitis.

Diverticulitis vs. diverticulosis

If you have diverticula that aren't infected or inflamed, it's known as diverticulosis.

Researchers report that in about 80 percent of cases, diverticulosis doesn't cause any symptoms. If you have diverticulosis without symptoms, you probably won't need treatment.

But in other cases, diverticulosis can cause symptoms such as pain in the abdomen and bloating. When that happens, it's known as symptomatic uncomplicated diverticular disease (SUDD).

About 4 percent of people with SUDD eventually develop diverticulitis.

Bladder diverticulitis

Diverticula can also develop in your bladder. This happens when the lining of your bladder forms pouches, poking through weak spots in your bladder's wall.

Sometimes bladder diverticula are present at birth. In other cases, they develop later in life. They can form when your bladder outlet is blocked or your bladder isn't working properly due to illness or injury.

If you have bladder diverticula that becomes inflamed, it's known as bladder diverticulitis. To treat bladder diverticulitis, your doctor might prescribe antibiotics and pain medications. They might also recommend surgery to repair the diverticula.

It's also possible for diverticulitis in your colon to affect your bladder. In severe cases, you might develop a fistula between your colon and bladder. This is known as a colovesical fistula. Find out what this condition involves.

Esophageal diverticulitis

Diverticula can potentially form in your esophagus, too. This occurs when pouches develop in your esophageal lining.

Esophageal diverticula are rare. When they do develop, it's usually slowly and over many years. As they grow, they can cause symptoms or complications such as:

- trouble swallowing

- pain when swallowing

- halitosis, or bad breath

- regurgitation of food and saliva

- pulmonary aspiration; breathing regurgitated food or saliva into your lungs

- aspiration pneumonia; developing a lung infection after breathing in food or saliva

If the diverticula become inflamed, it's known as esophageal diverticulitis.

To treat esophageal diverticulitis, your doctor might prescribe antibiotics and pain medications. To repair the diverticula, they might recommend surgery. Get more information about your treatment options.

Diverticulitis and alcohol

In the past, some studies suggested that drinking alcohol might increase your risk of diverticulitis. But other studies have found no such link.

According to a review of research published in 2017, there's no strong evidenceTrusted Source that drinking alcohol raises your risk of this disease.

If you drink alcohol, your doctor will likely encourage you to drink in moderation only. Although alcohol consumption might not cause diverticulitis, drinking too much can raise your risk of many other health problems.

Takeaway

Diverticulitis is relatively common in the Western world. In most cases, it can be treated through short-term dietary changes and medication.

But if complications develop, they can be very serious. If you have complicated diverticulitis, your doctor will likely advise you to get treatment in a hospital. You might need to undergo surgery to repair damage to your colon.

If you have diverticulitis or questions about your risk of developing it, speak with your doctor. They can help you learn how to treat this disease and support your digestive health.

Foods to Avoid If You Have Diverticulitis

Diverticulitis is a type of disease that affects your digestive tract. It's a serious medical condition that causes inflamed pouches in the lining of your intestine. These pouches are called diverticula. They develop when weak spots in your intestinal wall give way under pressure, causing sections to bulge out.

In most cases, the pouches occur in the large intestine, which is also called your colon. Diverticula often exist without infection or inflammation. This condition is called diverticulosis, a less serious condition than diverticulitis. Diverticulosis becomes more common as you age, occurring in about half of Americans over age 60.

With diverticulitis, these diverticula are inflamed or infected, or they may tear. Diverticulitis may lead to serious health problems or complications, including:

- nausea

- fever

- severe abdominal pain

- bloody bowel movements

- abscess, or an inflamed pocket of tissue

- fistula

Your diet can affect your symptoms of diverticulitis. Read on to learn about certain foods you might want to avoid, and how your diet should vary when you're having symptoms and when you're not.

What foods should I avoid if I have an acute bout of diverticulitis?

Because the exact root cause of diverticulitis isn't yet known, there's no list of foods that are known to ease symptoms of this condition. Also, the National Institutes of Health states that you don't need to avoid certain foods if you have diverticulitis.

However, you may want to consider keeping certain foods to a minimum. Talk to your doctor about whether you should avoid the following foods or reduce the amounts you consume.

High-FODMAP foods

Research has found that a diet that limits foods that are high in FODMAPs — fermentable oligosaccharides, disaccharides, monosaccharides, and polyols — can benefit people with irritable bowel syndrome. Researchers have suggested people with diverticulitis may also benefit from this diet.

Some examples of foods high in FODMAPs include:

- certain fruits, such as apples, pears, and plums

- dairy foods, such as milk, yogurt, and ice cream

- fermented foods, such as sauerkraut or kimchi

- beans

- cabbage

- Brussels sprouts

- onions and garlic

High-fiber foods

Foods that are high in fiber may be helpful for people with diverticulosis who aren't having an acute flare up and may even help prevent diverticulitis in the first place.

A 2017 systematic review of studies on diverticulosis and the occurrence of acute diverticulitis showed a "reduction of abdominal symptoms and the prevention of acute diverticulitis" with the intake of fiber.

However, every individual is different, and your specific fiber needs will vary based on your condition and symptoms. If you're having pain or other symptoms, your doctor may suggest that you limit your intake of these foods for a while.

Fiber adds bulk to stool and may increase peristalsis or colon contractions. This may be painful and uncomfortable if you're having a flare up.

Avoiding high-fiber foods, particularly if you're inflamed, may ease symptoms and give your system a temporary rest. In addition, whether including higher or lower amounts of fiber, you should also drink plenty of water.

Fiber-rich foods you might want to limit or avoid, especially during a flare up, include:

• beans and legumes such as navy beans, chickpeas, lentils, and kidney beans

• whole grains such as brown rice, quinoa, oats, amaranth, spelt, and bulgur

• vegetables

- fruits

Foods high in sugar and fat

A standard diet high in fat and sugar and low in fiber may be linked with an increased incidence of diverticulitis. Research suggests that avoiding the following foods may help prevent diverticulitis or reduce its symptoms:

- red meat

- refined grains

- full-fat dairy

- fried foods

Other foods to avoid

In the past, doctors recommended that people with diverticulitis avoid eating nuts, popcorn, and most seeds.

It was thought that the tiny particles from these foods might get lodged in the pouches and lead to an infection.

More recently, most doctors have moved away from this advice. Modern researchTrusted Source has shown no evidence linking those foods with increased diverticular issues.

Some research has also suggested that people with diverticulitis avoid alcohol.

What foods should I eat if I have diverticulitis?

Treatment and disease management approaches for diverticulitis vary from person to person. However, your doctor will likely suggest that you adopt certain dietary changes to make the condition easier to tolerate and less likely to worsen over time.

If you're having an acute attack of diverticulitis, your doctor may suggest either a low-fiber diet or a clear liquid diet to help relieve your symptoms. They may recommend following one of these diets until you've recovered.

Low-fiber foods

Low-fiber foods to consider eating if you have symptoms of diverticulitis include:

- white rice, white bread, or white pasta, but avoid gluten-containing foods if you're intolerant

- dry, low-fiber cereals

- processed fruits such as applesauce or canned peaches

- cooked animal proteins such as fish, poultry, or eggs

- olive oil or other oils

- yellow squash, zucchini, or pumpkin: peeled, seeds removed, and cooked

- cooked spinach, beets, carrots, or asparagus

- potatoes with no skin

- fruit and vegetable juices

Clear liquid diet

A clear liquid diet is a more restrictive approach to relieving diverticulitis symptoms. Your doctor may prescribe it for a short period of time. A clear liquid diet usually consists of:

- water

- ice chips

- ice pops with frozen fruit puree or pieces of finely chopped fruit

- soup broth or stock

- gelatin, such as Jell-O

- tea or coffee without any creams, flavors, or sweeteners

- clear electrolyte drinks

Other dietary considerations

Whether on a clear liquid diet or not, it's generally helpful to drink at least eight cups of fluid daily. This helps keep you hydrated and supports your gastrointestinal health.

Be sure to talk with your doctor before making any dramatic dietary changes. After your condition improves, your doctor may recommend slowly adding low-fiber foods back into your diet. Once you no longer have symptoms of diverticulitis, your doctor may suggest that you resume a balanced diet.

Does a high-fiber diet reduce risk of diverticulitis?

Even though avoiding high-fiber foods can help relieve symptoms of diverticulitis, research has shown that regularly consuming a high-fiber diet with lots of vegetables, fruits, and whole grains may reduce the risk for acute diverticulitis.

Since fiber can soften your body's waste material, softer stool passes through your intestines and colon more quickly and easily. This, in turn, reduces the pressure in your digestive system, which helps prevent the formation of diverticula, as well as the development of diverticulitis.

A high-fiber diet is often one of the first things a doctor will recommend if you have diverticulosis or you've recovered from diverticulitis.

If you're not already consuming high-fiber foods, be sure to start slow when adding them to your diet. One study found that those who consumed at least 25 grams of fiber per day had a 41 percent lower risk for developing diverticular disease, compared with those who only consumed 14 grams.

For people without diverticular issues, eating a diet that's rich in fiber helps promote a healthy digestive system.

Research also shows that gut bacteria play a role in diverticular disease. Though more research is needed, future studies are likely to support the modulation of gut bacteria through a high-fiber diet and probiotic supplementation.

Talk with your doctor

If you've been given a diagnosis of diverticulitis, talk with your doctor about your food needs and food restrictions. It's important to discuss how food may heal and possibly aggravate your condition.

In general, if you have diverticulosis but you're not having a diverticulitis episode, a diet high in fiber will help prevent future flare-ups. Depending on the severity of an acute diverticulitis flare-up, a diet low in fiber or a clear liquid diet may be beneficial to reduce symptoms.

If you need additional guidance, ask your doctor to refer you to a dietitian. Specifically, seek out a healthcare professional who has experience working with people who have diverticulitis. They can help you find ways to enjoy the high-fiber foods you need in your diet.

In addition, stay in communication with your doctor about your condition. While diverticulitis may remain dormant for long periods of time, keep in mind that it's a chronic, lifelong condition.

If you start to notice your symptoms increasing, have a plan of action ready from your doctor that can reduce pain and discomfort and help you manage your condition.

Diverticulitis Surgery

Why should I have diverticulitis surgery?

Diverticulitis surgery is usually done if your diverticulitis is severe or life-threatening. You can usually manage your diverticulitis by doing the following:

- taking prescribed antibiotics

- using nonsteroidal anti-inflammatory drugs (NSAIDs), such as ibuprofen (Advil)

- drinking fluids and avoiding solid food until your symptoms go away

Your doctor may recommend surgery if you have:

- multiple severe episodes of diverticulitis uncontrolled by medications and lifestyle changes

- bleeding from your rectum

- intense pain in your abdomen for a few days or more

- constipation, diarrhea, or vomiting that lasts longer than a few days

- blockage in your colon keeping you from passing waste (bowel obstruction)

- a hole in your colon (perforation)

- signs and symptoms of sepsis

What are the types of diverticulitis surgery?

The two main types of surgery for diverticulitis are:

- Bowel resection with primary anastomosis: In this procedure, your surgeon removes any infected colon (known as a colectomy) and sews together the cut ends of the two healthy pieces from either side of the previously infected area (anastomosis).

- Bowel resection with colostomy: For this procedure, your surgeon performs a colectomy and connects your bowel through an opening in your abdomen (colostomy). This opening is called a stoma. Your surgeon may do a colostomy if there's too much colon inflammation. Depending upon how well you recover over the next few months, the colostomy may be either temporary or permanent.

Each procedure can be done as open surgery or laparoscopically:

- Open: Your surgeon makes a six- to eight-inch cut in your abdomen to open your intestinal area to view.

- Laparoscopic: Your surgeon makes only small cuts. The surgery is accomplished by placing small cameras and instruments into your body through small tubes (trocars) that are usually less than one centimeter in size.

What are the risks associated with this surgery?

As with any surgery, your risk of complications may be increased if you:

- are obese

- are over the age of 60

- have other significant medical conditions such as diabetes or high blood pressure

- have had diverticulitis surgery or other abdominal surgery before

- are in overall poor health or not getting enough nutrition

- are having emergency surgery

How do I prepare for this surgery?

A few weeks before your surgery, your doctor may ask you to do the following:

• Stop taking medications that may thin your blood, such as ibuprofen (Advil) or aspirin.

• Stop smoking temporarily (or permanently if you're ready to quit). Smoking can make it harder for your body to heal after surgery.

• Wait for any existing flu, fever, or cold to break.

• Replace most of your diet with liquids and take laxatives to empty your bowels.

In the 24 hours before your surgery, you may also need to:

- Only drink water or other clear liquids, such as broth or juice.

- Not eat or drink anything for a few hours (up to 12) before the surgery.

- Take any medications that your surgeon gives you right before surgery.

Make sure you take some time off work or other responsibilities for at least two weeks to recover in the hospital and at home. Have someone ready to take you home once you're released from the hospital.

How is this surgery done?

To perform a bowel resection with primary anastomosis, your surgeon will:

1. Cut three to five small openings in your abdomen (for laparoscopy) or make a six- to eight-inch opening to view your intestine and other organs (for open surgery).

2. Insert a laparoscope and other surgical tools through the cuts (for laparoscopy).

3. Fill your abdominal area with gas to allow more room to do the surgery (for laparoscopy).

4. Look at your organs to make sure there aren't any other issues.

5. Find the affected part of your colon, cut it from the rest of your colon, and take it out.

6. Sew the two remaining ends of your colon back together (primary anastomosis) or open a hole in your abdomen and attach the colon to the hole (colostomy).

7. Sew up your surgical incisions and clean the areas around them.

Are there any complications associated with this surgery?

Possible complications of diverticulitis surgery include:

- blood clots

- surgical site infection

- hemorrhage (internal bleeding)

- sepsis (an infection throughout your body)

- heart attack or stroke

- respiratory failure requiring the use of a ventilator for breathing

- heart failure

- kidney failure

- narrowing or blockage of your colon from scar tissue

- formation of an abscess near the colon (bacteria-infected pus in a wound)

- leaking from area of anastomosis

- nearby organs getting injured

- incontinence, or not being able to control when you pass stool

How long does it take to recover from this surgery?

You'll spend about two to seven days in the hospital after this surgery while your doctors monitor you and make sure you can pass waste again.

Once you go home, do the following to help yourself recover:

- Don't exercise, lift anything heavy, or have sex for at least two weeks after you leave the hospital. Depending on your preoperative status and how your surgery went, your doctor may recommend this restriction for longer or shorter periods of time.

- Have only clear liquids at first. Slowly reintroduce solid foods into your diet as your colon heals or as your doctor instructs you to.

- Follow any instructions you were given for taking care of a stoma and colostomy bag.

What's the outlook for this surgery?

The outlook for diverticulitis surgery is good, especially if the surgery is done laparoscopically and you don't need a stoma.

See your doctor right away if you notice any of the following:

- bleeding from your closed cuts or in your waste

- intense pain in your abdomen

- constipation or diarrhea for more than a few days

- nausea or vomiting

- fever

You may be able to have a stoma closed a few months after surgery if your colon heals fully. If a large section of your colon was removed or if there's a high risk of reinfection, you may need to keep a stoma for many years or permanently.

While the cause for diverticulitis is unknown, making healthy lifestyle changes may curb it from developing.

Eating a high-fiber diet is one recommended way to help prevent diverticulitis.

How to Eat (and Recover from) a Low-Fiber Diet

What's a low-fiber diet?

A low-fiber diet (also called a restricted-fiber diet) limits the amount of high-fiber foods you eat each day. This helps give your digestive system a rest. A low-fiber diet should:

• reduce the amount of undigested food moving through your intestines and bowels

• ease the amount of work your digestive system isn't doing

• reduce the amount of stool you produce

• ease abdominal pain, diarrhea, and other symptoms

Only eat a low-fiber diet if your doctor tells you to. This is often to treat symptoms like diarrhea and cramping, before colonoscopies, after certain surgeries, or if you have a flare-up of one of the following gut issues:

- irritable bowel syndrome

- diverticulitis

- Crohn's disease

- ulcerative colitis

This diet is restricting, nutritionally limiting, and not intended for weight loss. If you don't do it right, it may cause more unintended side effects and symptoms in the long run. Read more to learn how to do a low-fiber diet right.

What can you eat on a low-fiber diet?

Typically, a low-fiber diet limits fiber intake to around 10 to 15 grams per day for both men and women. A low-fiber diet is made up of foods you shouldn't eat in large quantities or rely on for your health. This includes white bread, ice cream, and protein. As long as you stick to a low-fiber diet for a short amount of time — until your bowels heal, diarrhea resolves, or you're healed from surgery — you'll be OK.

Low-fiber foods

- white bread

- white pasta

- white rice

- foods made with refined white flour, like pancakes

- low-fiber hot and cold cereal

- eggs

- well-cooked canned or fresh vegetables in small amounts

- potatoes without the skin

- fats like olive oil, mayonnaise, gravy, and butter

- dairy products if you can tolerate them

- tender protein sources like eggs, tofu, chicken, and fish

- creamy peanut butter

Low-fiber fruits

- fruit juices without pulp

- canned fruit

- bananas

- cantaloupe
- honeydew melon
- watermelon
- nectarines
- papayas
- peaches
- plums

Low-fiber vegetables

- well-cooked or canned vegetables without seeds or skins
- carrots
- beets
- asparagus tips

- white potatoes without skin

- string beans

- lettuce if you can tolerate it

- tomato sauces

- acorn squash without seeds

- pureed spinach

- strained vegetable juice

You may eat cucumbers without seeds or skin, zucchini, and shredded lettuce raw.

Any food that you know is difficult for your system to handle should also be avoided. When you're going on a low-fiber diet, certain foods — like spicy foods — may affect your digestive system more. Tea, coffee, and alcohol may need to be avoided during this time.

Foods to avoid

- onions and garlic

- potatoes with skin left on

- bran

- raw or cooked cruciferous vegetables

- raw and dried fruit

- beans, lentils, nuts, and seeds

- whole grain foods

- wild or brown rice

- anything spicy, fried, or tough

- processed or tough meat

Ask your doctor about these foods and any other foods you're wondering about before you begin the diet. Also make a point to keep your fluid intake high. This will help you avoid constipation while on this diet plan.

Always talk to your doctor about your specific needs and the type of plan which will most benefit your overall health before you hit the grocery store. Make sure to read labels and avoid any food that contains more than 1 gram of fiber.

You can also meet with a dietitian for specific meal plans and guidance on eating a low-fiber diet.

Need a starting point?

Breakfast: Try scrambled eggs with buttered white toast and vegetable juice.

Lunch: Have a tuna salad sandwich on an unseeded white roll with half a banana.

Dinner: Make a piece of lightly seasoned, broiled salmon with mashed potatoes.

Why is a low-fiber diet beneficial?

You should only go on a low-fiber diet if your doctor tells you to. Your doctor may recommend this diet if you have:

- inflammatory bowel disease

- Crohn's disease

- ulcerative colitis

- diverticulitis

- diarrhea

- abdominal cramps

- constipation

- trouble with digestion

- irritation or damage in your digestive tract

- narrowing of the bowel caused by a tumor

- post-surgical recuperation from gastrointestinal procedures like colostomy and ileostomy

- gone through radiation or other types of treatments which might affect your gastrointestinal tract

You may also need to eat a low-fiber diet for 2 to 3 days prior to getting a colonoscopy.

How to start eating fiber again

Once you've reset your digestive system, you should slowly return to eating fiber-rich foods by introducing a small portion of one fiber food per day. If the food doesn't cause symptoms within 24 hours, it can be added to your diet.

Avoid eating all your fiber in one sitting or meal. The best way to get lots of it is by eating fruits with skins left on, raw vegetables, whole grains, beans, nuts, and seeds.

Know your fibers

There are two types of fiber:

- Soluble fiber foods absorb water during digestion, which turns them into a soft, gel-like substance. Soluble fiber foods, like apples, peas, or beans, are less irritating to the digestive tract and can often be eaten in small amounts.

- Insoluble fiber foods don't dissolve completely in the stomach. The small bits of undigested food that remain can be irritating to the intestines. On a low-fiber diet, you'll have to be especially careful to avoid foods like whole wheat, grains, and raw veggies.

Takeaway

Only eat a low-fiber diet if your doctor has recommended it. Your doctor will be able to tell you how long you need to be on the diet. It'll depend on your situation or condition.

Work with a dietitian to create an individualized plan. During your low-fiber diet, avoid foods that have insoluble fiber and be sure to take note of the fiber content in packaged foods.

Many of the foods allowed on a low-fiber diet, like pudding and white bread, shouldn't become a staple to your regular diet, especially after you start slowly reintroducing fiber.

Dietary fiber sources	Fiber content (g/100 g edible food portion)
Couscous, dry	5.00
Rice flour, brown	4.80
Broadbeans, immature seeds, raw	4.20
Hemp seeds, hulled	4.00
Squash, winter, hubbard, raw	3.90
Grapes, muscadine, raw	3.90
Brussels sprout, raw	3.80
Mushrooms, chanterelle, raw	3.80
Seeds, pumpkin and squash seed kernels, roasted, with salt added	3.88
Beet greens, raw	3.70

Pine nuts, raw	3.70
Cranberries, raw	3.60
Cashew nuts, raw	3.30
Cauliflower, green, raw	3.20
Okra, raw	3.20
Turnip greens, raw	3.20

Broccoli, cooked, boiled, drained, without salt 3.24

Pears, raw	3.10
Cabbage, savoy, raw	3.10
Chicory, witloof, raw	3.10
Endive, raw	3.10
Fennel, bulb, raw	3.10

Waterchestnuts, chinese, (matai), raw 3.00

Eggplant, raw 3.00

Kiwifruit, green, raw 3.00

Carrots, baby, raw 2.90

Figs, raw 2.90

Beets, raw 2.80

Carrots, raw 2.80

Mushrooms, morel, raw 2.80

Mustard spinach, (tendergreen), raw 2.80

Beans, snap, green, raw 2.70

Corn, sweet, white, raw 2.70

Mushrooms, enoki, raw 2.70

Mushrooms, maitake, raw 2.70

Banana, raw 2.60

Broccoli, raw 2.60

Peas, edible-podded, raw 2.60

Cabbage, raw 2.50

Chives, raw 2.50

Mushrooms, shiitake, raw 2.50

Mountain yam, hawaii, raw 2.50

Potatos, raw, skin 2.50

Blueberries, raw 2.40

Oranges, raw, Florida 2.40

Potatoes, white, flesh and skin, raw 2.40

Mushrooms, oyster, raw 2.30

Plantains, green, raw 2.20

Bamboo shoots, raw 2.20

Spinach, raw 2.20

Asparagus, raw 2.10

Cabbage, red, raw 2.10

Lettuce, cos or romaine, raw 2.10

Printed in Great Britain
by Amazon